This journal is presented to

_____

From _____

Date _____

A Special Note

UNSTOPPABLE
PRAISE

Though He Slay Me, Yet Will I Hope in Him

Journal
WITH QUOTES
FROM THE 14 CATEGORIES OF POEMS

Myrlande Joseph

Copyright © 2020 by Myrlande Joseph

All rights reserved.

This journal or any portion thereof may not be reproduced or used in any manner whatsoever without the express written permission of the publisher, except for the use of brief quotations in a book review.

Printed in the United States of America
First Printing, 2020
ISBN: 978-1-7354400-3-3

Scriptures taken from the Holy Bible, New International Version® NIV®. Copyright © 1973, 1978, 1984, 2011 by Biblica, Inc.® Used by Permission of Biblica, Inc.® All rights reserved worldwide.

Message for You, the Journal-Writer

Dear Writer,

Writing about God, testifying on His behalf, praising and worshiping Him, and serving the poor are my greatest loves. Writing is the medium through which I feel most free to express my deepest thoughts and feelings. It is also where I find peace and trust in God in whatever trial I am experiencing.

I hope the unique quotes from my book Unstoppable Praise will not only positively affect your life but will also draw you nearer to God through worship. I also hope that, as you begin to praise and worship Him, God will reveal Himself to you and you will record every fresh word, idea, vision, and revelation down in this journal.

Blessings,
Myrlande Joseph

Then the LORD replied: "Write down the revelation and make it plain on tablets so that a herald may run with it."

—Habakkuk 2:2 (NIV)

Praise and Worship Quotes

"Sometimes I wonder why I praise Thee, O LORD."

*"Wait a minute! I think I know why!
You breathed life into me today!
And your Word says,
"Let everything that has breath praise the Lord!"*

"I made up my mind to give Him praise and worship Him."

> "He deserves our praise at all times—
> Not just when everything is going well for us,
> But also in bad times."

"It's okay if I don't have it all on this day"

"Truly, none of these things matter.
What matters most is that I have Your breath in me
To worship You day and night
And glorify Your name above all names."

"It's okay that the condition is still the same
And that I am still dreaming and hoping,
Waiting to see Your glory manifest in my life,
Waiting to see myself before great men,
Waiting to see Your name glorified in my life.
Yet, Lord, I will still praise You
And magnify Your holy name."

"The delay is too small to keep me from praising You."

"All the storms of life are too small to stop me from praising You."

*"The rejections and snubs are too small
To keep me from glorifying Your name."*

"The unfulfilled dreams are too small to stop me from exalting You."

"The desires are too small to impede me from blessing You."

"For I am convinced
That neither a car,
A home,
A husband,
Wealth,
Possessions,
Delays,
Unanswered prayers,
Or unfulfilled dreams
Will be able to stop me
From blessing Your name."

"I may not have it all today.
I may still wait
For the dreams to come to pass
I may still wait
To fulfill my destiny.
But I have You, Lord."

"If I have You, I have everything in You."

"O, how I long each day to shout, "Hallelujah,"
Making sound in Your ear,
Singing fresh and new melodies to You each day,
Praising You and magnifying Your name."

*"O God, my Lord, my Salvation,
How I love to praise Your Holy name,
Exalt it every day and night!"*

"Today, I worship You, O God.
Right in the midst of my storms I glorify Your name."

"Truly only He deserves the praise, the glory, and the honor.
Therefore, I must give them back to Him—
Not some, but all the praise and glory."

"If I had let my emotions control me when I woke up this morning, You would not get this praise today."

"Again, I did not praise You today because my situation changed, And I am where I want to be in life."

"I didn't praise You because my prayers were answered
Or I saw the husband next to me when I woke up today."

"I didn't praise You because I have wealth, riches or possessions."

> "I praised You because I love you,
> And I desire to bless Your name that is above all names."

*"I love to praise that name—
His name that is a strong tower."*

"O, how I love to lift that name up,
And exalt it before men, blessing it day and night!"

*"O, how I long to bless that name forever and ever,
That name that is the way, the truth and the life,
And giving it an unstoppable praise, forever praised!"*

"O, how I love to praise that name, Jesus!"

"He whispered, "Are you out of your mind? Don't you have anything better to do with your life? Why still praise Him?"

> "Forever I will bow down and worship Him,
> For He is worthy of praise."

"He deserves it day and night, in good and bad times."

> "Again, it doesn't matter, Father of Lies.
> I will worship Him anyway, for my God is not dead!"

"I may not be where I want to be,
But I am not who I used to be twenty years ago."

"Lord, I don't need to be where I want to be today to give You praise."

"My situation doesn't need to turn around to give You praise."

"My condition doesn't need to change to give You praise."

"I will give You praise right where I am,
In the silence,
In my dead situation,
In the confusion,
In the unknown."

"*Hallelujah, Glory be to Your name, Jesus, My Lord, my salvation!*"

"O God of Abraham, Isaac, and Jacob,
I give You praise
Right in the middle of the storm."

"O, how I long to see my King,
How I long to worship Him for eternity,
My Lord and my salvation,
The one who reigns forever and ever!"

"Yes, on this day, I will bless Him and magnify the Lord. I will exalt Him, too, for He has been good to me."

"Indeed, no one is eligible or qualified to receive this very praise."

*"Truly, my God is worthy of this praise.
No one qualifies or is worthy of it
But my Father, who is my rock,
My deliverer, my provider, and my healer."*

"Why one day?
Aren't there 365 days in a year?

"I think He's too good
And too awesome of a King to be celebrated just one day."

"I think He should be remembered more often."

"All I want, all I desire is to be with Him in paradise!"

Homelessness Quotes

*"I want to go home to a place
Where I don't have to rush to get up from where I lay
And stay there, worshipping Him all day long."*

"Lord, I want to go home to that place again,
That place I once have called home
That was taken from me suddenly."

*"Please, Lord, take me home one more time.
I want to go home."*

*"Trust me when I say I know,
I understand and can relate."*

*"I know what it's like to be homeless
And find yourself in random places."*

"So, please don't be fooled by my nice attire.
You have no idea what I've been through."

"So trust me when I say
I know what it's like to be you."

*"I may not have a home now,
I may not have wealth, possessions, or status,
But one thing I know:
I am rich!"*

> "I may not look like one in your definition of prosperity.
> I may not look like one in your definition of success.
> My condition may speak louder
> Than the very word coming out of my mouth:
> That I am rich.
> But believe me when I say,
> I am rich!"

*"I wonder when this struggle will end?
For I want to be set free and delivered from homelessness."*

"I don't know what to do to get some sleep. Jesus! I need some sleep to concentrate."

"I want to be set free from homelessness."

"When will be the day I see myself home again?"

Waiting and Giving Up Quotes

> "Truly, I can't rely on any man,
> For many have given me false hopes
> And never fulfilled their promises to me."

"I want to break free from them today
And see what's on the other side of them."

*"Who would have thought, at my age,
Today I would still be in this condition,
Stuck and unable to move forward?"*

"Then again, maybe I am not being punished for any of them."

"Maybe I'm just like Job, where God is asking Satan,
"Do you consider my servant Myrlande?"
Or maybe God is up to something
And getting ready to blow some minds
As He told me not too long ago."

"Therefore, I will wait on Him
And watch Him make a way for me
To exit these prison walls."

*"Lord, it has been some time
Since You brought change in my condition,
Since I last saw Your glory
And tasted Your goodness."*

"For some time now
I have been on the lookout,
Hoping the phone will ring with good news,
Hoping my email will fill with good news."

"I don't recall You ever being this late."

*"You have always been present in my trouble
When I called upon You."*

*"Now, since I don't understand
The reason for this delay,
Please help me to trust Your timing."*

"I refuse to settle!"

"Believe me, it's too late for that,
When I know the power is within me,
When I know the earth is His and everything in it,
The world and all who live in it."

"Why should I settle
When I have already experienced His power
And witnessed it in other's lives?"

"I think it's a little too late to settle for less."

"Believe me, it's too late to settle now.
It's too late to settle for less."

*"So, I refuse to settle,
But to wait on the Lord."*

> *"Why now, soul? Why give up now?*
> *Have you forgotten who He is?"*

"Why now, soul?
Why feel discouraged within me?
Why want to give up when He is not dead?"

"It wasn't long ago
When He made a way out of no way for me,
When He shifted things in my favor
And put a smile on my face."

*"Last time I checked,
He was the same miracle God
And the same deliverance God."*

"Why give up now when the condition is temporary?"

Alone And Forsaken, Hopeless, Helplessness Quotes

"Though He seems invisible, I am not alone,
For He lives in me, and I in Him."

"Don't be fooled by my condition
Where I am stuck
And can't find anybody to come and rescue me."

"I am not alone; I am not forsaken."

> "In the midst of my trials, He is there.
> In the midst of my loneliness, He is there.
> In the midst of my storms, He is there.
> In the midst of my sorrows, He is there.
> I'm not alone and never will be."

"This is not the life I dreamed of after coming to America. This is not the life I envisioned after college."

*"I never thought at my age
I would be sleeping at someone else's home
With no source of income."*

"This was never the life I envisioned after giving my life to Him. This was never the life I dreamed of after graduate school."

*"I never thought at my age
I would jump from one place to another.
I never thought at my age I would crash at a friend's place."*

"Why won't He let me go
When nothing is happening for me?
Does that mean He's not done yet with me?"

"Could there still be hope for me after all these years?"

"O Spirit of God, move!
I am stuck and can't find a way out.
I am trapped and can't move forward.
I am lost and can't be found by anyone."

"Don't let them question Your ability to help me."

"Don't let them doubt your power that is in me
To accomplish all things and become all things.
So, Holy Spirit, move on my behalf on this day!
Come like a flood, and help me get to my destiny!"

"I miss You, Daddy!
Please help me find my way back into Your presence,
Singing praises to You,
Blasting praise and worship music once more."

"O how my soul longs for fellowship with my Father! O how I miss our intimacy!"

"Help me to fully know that You love me unconditionally. Nothing I do can separate me from Your love."

"Please, Father, help me!
Deliver me from all unrighteousness,
Set me free from this state of depression,
Set me free from loneliness,
Set me free from oppression,
Set me free from the darkness of this world."

*"I need Your very strength and power
To rise again and be in Your presence."*

"I need your very Spirit to help me get back on track."

*"Please take hold of me this evening
And lead me into your presence,
For I miss you very much."*

*"All I want and desire
Is to do what's right in Your sight."*

"It's true, Lord.
Your glory is what I desire
To see manifested in my life."

"Show me the way to go,
For I want to see You like never before."

Unnoticed, Rejected, and Overlooked

"For years I was invisible in their sights.
For years I cried out loud,
And they still didn't notice me."

*"I tried everything I could think of
Just to get their attention."*

"I know, I know what it's like to be humiliated, Overlooked, forsaken, and rejected."

"I used every gifts and talents to impress them."

*"It's just not the season yet.
It's just not the time yet.
When the time is right,
Who will be able to overlook you?"*

"For years, I waited to be noticed."

"For years, I waited to be somebody in their eyes."

"I waited and waited for one to at least notice me,
But no one did."

"Let them overlook you."

"Hang in there!
God knows what He's doing."

*"If you only knew who I was,
You would not have skipped me."*

*"If you only knew what I made up,
You would not have overlooked me."*

"Why are you letting the outward appearance fool you?"

"Sometimes I wonder, are you truly connected to Him? Do you truly understand how He operates?"

"I may not have the five years' experience,
But I have His ability to do all things,
Just as I am currently doing free labor."

*"Don't be fooled by my lack of experience,
Thinking I don't have what it takes."*

"Who are you to say I'm not talented enough?"

*"Who are you to say that I'm not qualified
When I have a helper that lives on the inside of me?"*

*"I do not need your approval,
For I know who I am and whose I am."*

"It is He who gives men special talents, skills,
And ability to glorify Him.
So, yes, I can do all things."

Suicidal Thoughts, Voices, and Negative Words Quotes

"Your hope is in the wrong thing."

"Your trust and confidence are in the wrong people."

"Chasing after the wrong thing is meaningless."

"You can't put your hope and trust in them.
You can't put your confidence in them.
You can't listen to them.
They will disappoint you in a split second."

"I don't know if you know this,

But you are not your own.

You belong to Him."

"Trust me, He is who He says He is.
He will never disappoint you,
Nor forsake you,
Nor look down on you."

*"If you put your confidence in him,
He will not disappoint you."*

"Hope without Him is death,
But hope in Him is life."

"That's right, I said it—
Get behind me."

"I know what you came to do:
You came to erase me from the face of the earth,
An earth that's not even yours,
An earth formed and established by my heavenly Father."

"Sorry, you can't have me.
Sorry, you can't destroy me.
I now know who I am and whose I am."

"I know what you came to do.
I know what you're trying to do.
Sorry, you've got the wrong person today."

"I was bought at a price. Therefore, get behind me, Father of Lies."

"I will not die
But live and fulfill my destiny.

*"I know what you came to do,
But you will not have me.
Not today, tomorrow, or ever.
So get behind me."*

"I will not leave this earth in this condition,
Nor will I stay in it any longer,
For all His promises to me are 'yes' and 'amen,'
And He is not a man who would lie
Nor a son of man who would change his mind."

"The plan was to destroy me for good,
Not to live to see this very day,
Writing to help save someone's life."

"Had you told me thirty years later,
I would still be breathing,
I would not have believed you."

*"Yes, I should have been dead,
But I am still standing by God's grace."*

"Liar! I will live my full potential."

"I am confident
That I will see my situation once more turn around."

"You, Father of Lies,

Last time I read,

It is in Him I live, move, and have my being."

Stress and Anxiety Quotes

"You have always been on time.
To the contrary, You always show yourself faithful
And You're never an hour late."

*"You have never failed to come to my rescue
Or make a way for me."*

"I don't remember ever having to wait for this long.
I don't remember You taking this long to answer me."

"Maybe I've lost track of what You've done in the past. Maybe I've taken my eyes off of You."

"When you say wait, I'm still.
Now, suddenly, I can't move forward?
No, I must trust you and get back on track."

> *"Trust me when I say
> It's not the end,
> And it's not too late."*

*"Trust me when I say it isn't over yet,
So be of good courage!"*

"It doesn't matter what it looks like.
It doesn't matter who is in the current position.
This is not the end."

"So today I encourage you to be of good courage
And know that the earth is His and everything in it."

"It's not too late for Him to turn it around. It's not too late for Him to bring change."

"Be of good courage!
It's not too late.
God can still bring it to pass."

"Holy Spirit,
Help this soul of mine be still
And know that my God is not a liar."

"Spirit of truth,
Help this soul of mine be still
And know that my Heavenly Father
Will never fail me."

*"Yes, Spirit of God,
Take control of my mind and rule over it."*

"I may not see a way out,
But that doesn't mean He doesn't have one."

*"Why are you panicking?
Why lose sleep worrying about tomorrow?"*

"Did He tell you He was done with you?"

"So why are you afraid?
Is there a situation He cannot turn around?
Is there a mountain He cannot move?"

"O you little doubter,
Where is your faith?"

*"You don't need to be anxious.
You don't need to worry.
God is working out the details of your life."*

"O soul, wake up!
Wake up and praise the Great King!"

"You must wake up and bless Him, for He has not changed."

"Wake up! Wake up! And worship Him!
You have no reason to feel down today."

*"Tell me, why be anxious
When He is with all powers in His hands?"*

"Why do you fret
When He reigns forever,
When He is the God of Glory,
The God of restoration,
And the God of justice?"

"Trust me when I say it's not over—
At least believe me when I say,
He has the power to turn it around for your good."

*"He is not limited by these results.
What just happened was not by accident."*

"Why lose hope when you can just trust Him with the plans He has for you?"

"Yes, the Lord is good indeed.
He gave me the ability
To accomplish everything set before me."

"Indeed, He is good."

"Not one of his promises fails to come to pass in my life."

"Yes, I sought the Lord with all my heart,
And He revealed Himself to me,
Not once, not twice,
But too many times to count."

"Truly the Lord can be found
If you seek Him with all your heart,
For my anxiety is no more,
My fears are gone,
My confusions are no more,
Situations turned around,
Chains loosened and broken."

Identity Crisis and Confusion Quotes

> *"Some say they know me,*
> *But have no idea who I am."*

*"They defined me by my past,
My present condition, and my status
But have no idea who He says I am."*

> "When they see me,
> They see two decades ago,
> Yesterday, ordinary, teen mom,
> Homeless, burden, poor,
> Unstable, unemployed, needy,
> And always struggling."

"When I look at you, I see set apart, chosen one,
My glory, purpose and destiny."

"You're not your own,
Nor do you belong to them.
You are mine."

"*You are my child, that's who you are!*"

> "In fact, I called you 'friend'
> And tell you great, unsearchable things
> You did not know."

"My God knows my name,
And always answers me when I call on Him."

*"O, how blessed I am to know the living God,
The great and magnificent God who reigns forever!"*

"Some said I'm amazing, smart, beautiful, and a Christian."

"Thrilled that this one is a man of God,
Thrilled that some are God-conscious men,
Could this one finally be the one? I thought."

"Then I wonder, what's wrong with me?

Why can't I keep a man?

Why are they leaving me suddenly?

Why they are disappearing so quickly?

Why they are rejecting me?

Am I cursed?"

"Then I heard a voice say, "No, my daughter,
Nothing is wrong with you.
Everything I made is good."

"Wow, I can't believe He loves me just the way I am!"

"I don't need to look a certain way for Him to love me."

"Gaining or losing weight, He still loves me.
Uptight or reserved, He still loves me.
Employed or unemployed, He still loves me.
He loves me just the way I am."

> "Yes, I'll say it again:
> He loves me just the way I am."

"Don't let their words confuse you;
He alone is mighty!"

*"I searched and couldn't find one
Who could make me walk in freedom."*

"Trust me when I say He is mighty,
For I know what it's like to be delivered and set free."

Unloved and Worthless Quotes

"Don't walk away yet!
There's no other one out there."

"A one of a kind,

Hidden treasure.

Who can find it?"

"A pure and passionate heart.
Who can find it out there?"

*"What choice do I have?
Don't good gifts come from You?"*

> "Many have disappointed me
> And failed to see the woman I am in you,
> The one of a kind you have created,
> The God-fearing and devoted woman,
> The loveable, caring,
> And compassionate woman I am in you"

"I've used them all just to impress them.
As you see, I have no more gifts left to use."

"Why waste my energy
Trying to find somebody
To look at me and validate me
When I already know that I am loved
By a King unconditionally?"

*"You don't need somebody
Who can't seem to understand your worth in Him."*

"You'd better wake up, self,
And understand your true worth in Him."

"You don't need somebody
Who thinks you are too holy for them,
When God Himself is Holy."

"Today, for the first time, I can honestly say that I am content with You."

> "I am no longer feeling unloved, unwanted, and worthless,
> For I am convinced that Your love is enough for me,
> And it is far greater than any human love."

Fear, Doubts, Worry Quotes

> "Have you not heard
> The Lord is the same
> From yesterday, today, and forever?"

*"Why are you worrying
About my tomorrows?"*

*"O you of little faith,
Did His nature change?
Did Jesus leave His right side
And His Spirit is no more?"*

*"Why are you doubting His ability
To make a way for me over the other side
When He just made a way for me
Right before your very own eyes?"*

"O you of little faith,
Is anything too hard for the Lord?"

> "Why are you worrying
> About my tomorrows
> When you can't even add
> An hour to them?"

> "It's not a question
> Whether He still performs miracles.
> Truly, it's about,
> Do you believe in the impossible?"

"I bet you don't know my name or my background
Because if you did,
You would not stop talking to me."

"Clearly you do not know my history

Because if you did,

You would not keep looking me up and down."

"Why stop interacting with me
When you still have your position?"

"Please don't let this chair I'm sitting on fool you
Or the glass door fool you."

> "I know that sitting behind the glass
> Can appear as though I have arrived.
> But allow me to tell you
> A little bit about me."

"Rest assured—

I'm just passing by.

I am not here looking for a title,

Nor am I here to rule over you."

"You don't have to worry—
I'm just here working for a greater purpose,
That is, saving money to fulfill my destiny."

"It was never my intention
To not fully trust You with all my heart
When You have proven Yourself to me
Day after day."

*"Truly You have done wonders in the past
And had revealed Yourself to me,
Even in my dead situations."*

"Lord, help me to fully trust You with the process And not lean on my own understanding."

"You may not understand the very words
That will come out of my mouth.
But I do know Him
And can testify about Him."

"Believe me, I know what I am talking about. For I have seen His very power at work in my life. Truly, I know the God I serve."

"I serve a God
Who goes before me
In battles day and night."

> "For I serve a God
> Who is the God of completion.
> When He starts, He finishes."

Love and Intimacy Quotes

"He might have been the first,

But just realizing now

That I was wrong the entire time."

*"Just realizing now how I missed the entire truth,
Acknowledging someone else
Who is nowhere to be found today."*

*"Truly, I didn't know what love was
Until I saw You that day."*

"I wonder how I failed to acknowledge You first."

> "He might have been the first,
> But just realizing now
> That You are my heart
> And my first true love,
> I love You, Lord!"

"O how blessed I was to have that dance with You today, Dad!"

"I loved and enjoyed Your presence."

"For once I had to let go of someone's hands.
I had no choice but to let them go
And bow down and worship You—
All because Your presence overtook me."

"It was in Your presence I felt most free, safe, and secured."

"Truly there's none like You, O God.
There's no one I can find
Who is faithful to all His promises."

"*Indeed, there is none like You.
No one can love me like You do.*"

"There's no doubt about it—
You are indeed beautiful, Lord."

*"I wonder where Your beauty
Can be displayed for the world to see
That You are the most beautiful King alive!"*

"I adore You, my beautiful King."

"Is there someone out there who, when they speak, they act?
And when they promise, they fulfill?"

*"I don't know about you,
But I have not found anybody like Him
Who is gracious and merciful."*

"I asked, but they couldn't give.
Indeed, no one is like Him."

> "It is You I love with all my mind,
> With all my soul,
> And with all my strength."

"Who can replace You,
My very source of strength and joy?"

"It is You I adore,
It's always been You
And will forever be You."

> "I love You, lover of my soul—
> My very breath of life."

"All I desire is to be in Your presence more."

> "If I could, I would praise You around the clock 24/7,
> But with a destiny to fulfill,
> It's not possible."

Victory and Justice Quotes

*"Did you really think I was one of your fraud victims
And didn't have one who stood behind me?"*

"I was never alone when you saw me that morning."

*"He was present before the transaction,
During the transaction,
And after the transaction.
I was never alone."*

"Sorry if you got it all twisted.
You just happened to mess with the wrong person,
A child of God."

"Victory is always mine."

> "I think you got the name mixed up.
> I think you got it all twisted."

"Clearly, we're not on the same page of the Holy Bible. Who can stand against Him?"

"In His name
I cannot be defeated,
I cannot be stuck,
Not in His book,
Nor on earth,
Nor in heaven."

*"I'm not sure if you've heard of Him before
Or even know His name.
But in case you don't know or forget about His nature,
Please allow me to tell you a little bit about Him."*

> "His name is, 'I AM,'
> The God who created heaven and earth."

"You're too small to stop the process."

"For once, use your common sense and wake up. You are too small to stop His plan!"

"Dead situation, have you heard of the dry bones in the valley?
Dead condition, have you heard of the dry bones in the valley?
Dead season, have you heard of the dry bones in the valley?"

*"You have no choice
But to come to life."*

> "I wasn't born to live in poverty.
> I wasn't born to live in mediocrity.
> I wasn't born to live in lack."

*"Hallelujah! It will not be long
Before the world will know my name
Including my Father's name, I AM WHO I AM, God."*

"I will soon dance again."

*"She never thought it could ever happen to her.
She did not know her emotion could be as powerful,
To where it controls her every move,
But she cried out to God for mercy,
And the Lord heard her and delivered her."*

"She once was stuck,
But He made a way for her to escape
With just a song of praise."

*"Yes, today,
She's free, indeed!"*

"You have heard correctly:

They are mighty to win and mighty to set you free."

"You don't need a number to call them.
Just call upon the name of the Lord,
And they will be there."

*"Who can be against me
When He speaks, He acts,
And when He promises, He fulfills?"*

"Have you not heard
That the world and everything in it belongs to Him,
Including you and your financial institution?"

"Truly, if God is for me, who can be against me?"

Thankfulness Quotes

*"Surely, I made up my mind to be glad on this day
And bless His name that is above all names
For His goodness in my life.
Yes, I will rejoice."*

> "Indeed, I made up my mind
> To rejoice on this day
> And enter into His gates with thanksgiving
> And into His courts with praise
> And approach His throne with boldness and confidence,
> Giving Him thanks for all He has done for me."

"You didn't have to renew my strength and mind on this day."

"Thank you that I am in my right mind this morning."

"Yes, Lord, it's true!
You didn't have to be near me when I called on You today."

"Thank you for my ability to praise and bless you In my present condition."

"I hunger and thirst for it.
For, apart from it,
I won't be, can't be, and will never be."

"Who can live without it?
Who can walk right without it?"

> "My daily bread is what I look forward
> To reading each day
> And receiving each day."

"Thank you, Lord, for more of You in my life today."

"Yes, Lord, it is indeed another day
You have made for me to give You praise,
Another day to see Your kingdom come in my life,
Another day to see Your will be done in my life
On earth and as it is in heaven."

"*Thank you for your divine protection over my life and loved ones.*"

"Thank You for the two decades of walking with You
And still standing tall
Through it all."

"Lord, I thank you that You're not yet done with me."

"Thank you for Your fresh anointing to accomplish all things."

Grace and Restoration Quotes

"How many are my kind who slept under the tunnel
In the cold weather last night?
And yet, You've blessed me with a warm place to stay."

"I try to explain it,
But I can't.
I try to understand it,
But I can't seem to comprehend it.
Again and again,
You kept blowing my mind
With Your goodness."

*"Really, Lord, who am I
That every day I'm seeing new favor,
Encounter, and mercy?"*

"Relax, He did not forsake me.
He did not abandon me."

"I understand not everyone can handle other's blessings,
I understand not everyone can rejoice when others are rejoicing,
But trust me when I say I can handle it."

"Yes, I can handle it
And have the grace to handle yours
With His grace, which is sufficient for me."

"Thank you, Lord, for Your grace."

"It will not be long when they will soon see
Your mighty hands at work in my life,
When they will soon discover
There is one greater on the inside of me,
And when they will soon see
Your glory manifesting itself in my life."

"O, how I believe!
How I believe, very soon,
They are going to know Your name,
The greatest name of all,
Whose daughter I am
And who fathered me."

"I look forward, O Lord, to seeing You Make a way out of no way for me today."

> "Yes, Lord, I look forward, O Lord,
> To seeing Your wonders manifest themselves in this famine
> That I may proclaim Your good."

*"Many didn't think this day was possible
When I would talk about my day at work."*

"Many didn't think it was possible
To get out of my situation some day."

*"Some thought I would never rise from the ashes.
Little did they know
God had a set time for me to be set free,
God had a set time for me to be delivered."*

"They did not see it coming,
But God saw it coming.
They did not see it coming,
But I saw it coming
Through the eyes of faith."

*"I don't blame you for asking me who's my husband
And what he does for a living.
For I know His grace can make you ask these questions."*

"If you only knew my condition a week ago,
You would not have been compelled to ask me this question."

*"It was just a week ago
When I was locked in a cage for half a decade
And waiting to be set free."*

"In case you don't know,
The chains had fallen off of me just a week ago."

"So, don't be fooled by my fine clothes. I had just been set free a week ago."

"This is the day the Lord has made.
I will testify about His goodness in my life,
For I am no longer the needy,
I am no longer on the couch,
I am no longer occupying someone's bed."

"I will proclaim what He has done for me,
How He set me free
From homelessness, shame,
Humiliation, and rejection
And how He restored me
To the way I was before."

"Believe it or not, I checked all the requirements,
And I did not find anyone who met them."

"Indeed, no one is eligible or qualified
To receive this very praise."

*"I was left alone
With no one to come to my rescue."*

*"Therefore, I will not give my praise to another
Nor bow down to worship anyone
But Him who is most worthy of praise,
And who restored my life."*

*"Yes, Lord! Yes, Lord! Yes, Lord!
Go ahead and have Your way in me."*

"I thank You for the new season of change,
The new ideas, concepts, knowledge,
Understanding, and revelations I will receive."

*"May Your Glory be revealed in my life
While You make all things new."*

"Thank You for new provisions and opportunities
That are coming my way today
And for making all things new!"

"I will extol the LORD at all times; his praise will always be on my lips."

—Psalm 34:1 (NIV)

www.ingramcontent.com/pod-product-compliance
Lightning Source LLC
Chambersburg PA
CBHW071217080526
44587CB00013BA/1407